DATE DUE			
NOV 30 '95			
DEC - 3 '97			
FEB 1 7 '00			
FE 2 4 '03			
APR 2 9 2003			

PLYMOUTH:
PILGRIMS' STORY OF SURVIVAL

Linda R. Wade

ROURKE ENTERPRISES, INC.
Vero Beach, FL 32964

Library of Congress Cataloging-in-Publication Data

Wade, Linda R.
   Plymouth: Pilgrims' story of survival / by Linda R. Wade.
   p. cm. – (Doors to America's past)

   Includes index.
   Summary: Describes the reasons that the Pilgrims traveled to the New World, their voyage on the Mayflower, the hardships of their first winter in the Plymouth settlement, and the harvest celebration remembered as the first Thanksgiving. Also describes Plimoth Plantation, a recreation of the original seventeenth-century settlement.
   ISBN 0-86592-469-4
   1. Pilgrims (New Plymouth Colony) – Juvenile literature. 2. Massachusetts – History – New Plymouth, 1620-1691 – Juvenile literature.
 [1. Pilgrims (New Plymouth Colony). 2. Massachusetts – History – New Plymouth, 1620-1691. 3. Thanksgiving Day.] I. Title II. Series.
F68.W15 1991
974.4'8202 – dc20   90-46095
                                                                          CIP
                                                                          AC

Acknowledgments

   Special thanks to the following people who provided pictures and information: Paula Fisher, Carolyn Travers and Troy Creane of Plimoth Plantation; Laurence Pizer and Eleanor Driver of the Pilgrim Hall Museum; and Coralee Lonardo, Director, Plymouth National Wax Museum. I am also grateful to Richard E. Hogue for his editing assistance.

Photo Credits

Plimoth Plantation, Plymouth, Massachusetts: cover, 1, 6, right 29, 32, 44
Plymouth National Wax Museum: 8, 14, 19, 23, 25, 38, 40, 45
Public Domain: 18, left 29, 36, 43

Table of Contents

Introduction

The story of the Pilgrims is a story of bravery and determination. It is the story of people who sought the freedom to worship God in their own way, not the way prescribed by the established church, the Church of England. They were called Separatists because they wanted to separate from the official church. At the time, the early 1600s, England's king was James I. He ordered the Separatists to be arrested and jailed. Finally, they had only two choices: either to conform to the king's religion, or to escape from England.

Many of the Separatists chose to leave. They become known as Pilgrims because of their many moves in search of religious tolerance. They first went to Holland, where they enjoyed several years of relative freedom. But they still dreamed of a place to raise their children as they saw fit, without either English or Dutch control.

The Separatists managed to secure a loan from a company of English merchants interested in developing trade in the New World. Protected by the charter that the businessmen got from the king, the Separatists sailed for America on a ship called the *Mayflower*. They were joined by other English people who had their own hopes of building a better life in the New World.

In spite of two false and troublesome attempts to start the journey, the Pilgrims were not discouraged. They finally set sail for America on September 6, 1620. What followed was a 67-day voyage filled with storms, near-shipwreck, illness, terror—and much prayer by the pious and psalm-singing Pilgrims.

Having survived the treacherous crossing of the Atlantic, 102 weary but brave colonists had no way of knowing that the worst was yet to come. Had it not been for the friendship of some Native Americans, the Pilgrim settlers' hardships would have been even greater.

The small shipload of determined freedom lovers who stepped ashore at Plymouth on December 16, 1620, came to be known as America's founders. Let's visit these Pilgrim colonists and follow their search for freedom. Let's relive the story of their survival, a story of perseverance against all odds.

Pilgrim reading his Bible

1

Leaving England

The story of the Pilgrims begins in the village of Scrooby, England, in the early 1600s. A religious conflict arose on how best to worship God. The official church, the Church of England, was headed by the king, James I. It had established many laws and religious rituals. All English people had to observe the practices. But some people believed in a simpler kind of worship, and in self-government in spiritual matters. In 1602, these dissenters chose to separate from the established church. Two of the Separatists' leaders, William Brewster and William Bradford, would one day lead a small group of their people to a place in the New World that they would call Plymouth. Brewster, an elder of the group, would become the religious leader of the Plymouth settlement. Bradford would serve as governor of the colony for 36 years.

Because Separatist groups were illegal in England, members of the Scrooby congregation were hunted and persecuted. To escape religious intolerance and arrest, some members decided to move to Holland. Their decision to move meant that they not only were Separatists, but also pilgrims, people who travel to distant places.

Separatists were put in jail for not observing the religious rituals of the Church of England.

Leaving England without permission was a serious step; it was illegal to emigrate without authority. The Separatists risked imprisonment, but in their hearts, they knew the risk was worth taking. They began to sell their homes and belongings in Scrooby.

To escape illegally to Holland, the Separatists had to deal with shipmasters in secret, but the shipmasters often proved greedy and untrustworthy. They would agree to transport the Separatists across the North Sea to Holland, then sell the information to the king's soldiers. As the Pilgrims would be boarding a ship, they'd be arrested.

Some family members were separated while spending time in jail; others were stranded in empty ports. It would be several months before the Separatists who chose to leave England finally were united in Amsterdam, Holland, their new home.

Before long, the Pilgrims were faced with a threat as dangerous as the English persecution had been. The Amsterdam Separatist congregation came to include not just the Scrooby Separatists, but other Separatist groups from England. Soon the congregation was beset with controversy and personal quarrels. To avoid the conflict, the Scrooby Pilgrims decided to move to the Dutch town of Leyden, 24 miles away.

Leyden proved far more agreeable to the practice of their religion, but the Separatists had to work hard to make a living. Foreigners were not given the best choice of jobs. Nonetheless, with time, the Separatists purchased land and built new homes. In fact, they became so much a part of Holland that some of them married the Dutch, and Separatist men went to sea on Dutch ships. Such involvement in Dutch life began to disturb the Separatist elders. They saw it as a weakening of their congregation and a loss of many of the English ties that they still cherished.

Elder Brewster had a new idea of where the Separatists could have religious freedom—and also remain English. He sent pamphlets to the Separatists who still remained in England, proclaiming, "As the King forces his will upon the people, there will be no more freedom in England. America is the promised land."

Brewster's ideas were also hotly discussed in every Separatist home and meeting in Leyden. People were divided on the question. Those against leaving for America spoke of the hardships and dangers. There would be a long sea voyage and a scarcity of food in the wilderness. And there would be Native Americans who, from imaginative tales that had been woven, would harm the newcomers. Not the least of the people's concerns was the cost, far greater than the group could afford.

But the Separatists had also heard many favorable reports of the New World from early explorations made there. The English had already settled Jamestown, Virginia in 1607. And several years later, John Smith, an English shipmaster, had sailed along the shores of what he called New England. He even had written a book about the promising new American frontier.

2
Leaving Holland

The Separatists called a day of prayer to be followed by a day of decision. When the vote was taken, the answer was yes. The Separatists would go to America. But then, other decisions had to be made. Where in America should the Pilgrims go? How many of them would go? How would they get there?

The Pilgrims decided to go to Virginia, where the English already had a settlement. But they would ask to live in a separate area, where they would be guaranteed freedom of worship.

The Pilgrims sent a representative to England to talk to the Virginia Company, which had a charter from the king to colonize parts of the New World. The company was seeking people to settle in America. After a variety of negotiations, the company was able to get the king's permission for the Separatists to leave. The Pilgrims were also granted freedom of worship in their new home.

At the same time, some other English businessmen, hoping to profit from trade in America, provided funds for the Pilgrims' journey and settlement. The Pilgrims agreed to repay the loan with goods from America. The terms of the agreement were harsh. The colonists would have to work for the merchants for seven years, fishing, lumbering, farming, and fur trading, to send products back to England. So great was the debt and so small the group of Pilgrims to pay it, that after seven years much money would still be owed. The colonists would then have to mortgage their property. It would be 28 years after their arrival before the Pilgrims would finally pay off their debt.

Who would go to the New World? Not all of the Leyden Separatists chose to leave, nor did whole families go. Less than 40 people, a small part of the community, elected to make the journey. Others would join the first group later if the colony in America succeeded.

Next, transportation had to be secured. The Separatists bought a vessel called the *Speedwell*. It would first take the Pilgrims from Holland to England. There the expedition would be joined by another ship, the *Mayflower*, and by a group of other English people, most of them not Separatists. Because the Separatists did not have a group large enough to fill both ships, the merchants opened the trip to other people interested in settling in America.

The Separatist group was living up to the name by which it later could commonly be known—Pilgrims. For now again, as once in Scrooby and then in Amsterdam, the group was on the move. Those who would be leaving Leyden sold their property. The whole community put much work and money into outfitting the *Speedwell.* Large supplies of food and equipment were needed, not just for the trip to America, but for establishing a colony there.

It was a prayerful parting, as the Pilgrims knelt and asked for divine protection and received a final blessing from their pastor, who would stay on with the Leyden community. And it was a sorrowful parting, for many loved ones and friends were being left behind for a future that could at best be uncertain. So touching and sad was the departure that even Dutch strangers cried, people who were just passing by the dock as the *Speedwell* was setting out.

After the *Speedwell* arrived in England, the final readying of the expedition was completed. Then there came the second farewell, no less emotional than the first. The expedition now consisted of two ships and more than 120 passengers, all mixing excitement with fear and

Kneeling Pilgrims praying before leaving Holland

sadness as they made ready to move into the great Atlantic. The expedition, however, was destined to return to shore twice, for the *Speedwell* raised distress signals: the ship was leaking badly. After repairs, the ships once again set sail, only to find the *Speedwell* leaking again. Back in port, an examination once again showed no visible signs of leaks. Some people suspected that the ship's master deliberately sabotaged the ship because he and his crew did not want to go to America.

Now, more decisions had to be made. The *Mayflower* couldn't hold the passengers from both ships, so 20 people and their belongings had to be loaded off and left behind. In the meantime, valuable time had been lost. Now, the passengers of the *Speedwell* would have to join the *Mayflower*. It was September, and, by leaving so late, the colonists would be met by winter when they landed in America. Nonetheless, the brave and determined Pilgrims decided to set out for the third time.

3

A Long Ocean Journey

September 6, 1620. Once again it was departure day. Once again the passengers said tearful good-byes and boarded the *Mayflower*. Once again, sails were hoisted. And once again passengers hugged the rails as they watched loved ones and England slip away. But this time, there would be no turning back.

On board were 102 passengers. Getting settled on the ship was difficult. The passengers, plus the ship's master, Christopher Jones, and his crew of 25 sailors, were crammed into a ship equipped to carry only half that many people. The *Mayflower* was only about 100 feet long and 25 feet wide. There were few cabins and bunks. Most sleeping quarters were below deck where the air was hot and humid.

The voyage began with choppy seas that tossed the little ship about, causing belongings to slide back and forth across the decks. Many passengers became seasick and hung their heads over the rails.

Routines had to be set up for feeding the passengers and crew and for handling other necessary chores.

Children, either sick or restless, had to be managed as best as could be.

The ship's progress depended completely on the wind. Only when the wind was gentle could the *Mayflower* make good time. When the wind was calm, the ship stood still. When there was a storm, the sails had to be rolled up so that the wind did not tear them to shreds.

The Pilgrims continuously prayed and expressed gratitude to God for His goodness and blessings. For inspiration, they listened to Bible stories of the deliverance of God's people from perilous journeys. There was Israel's miraculous crossing of the Red Sea; Noah and his ark surviving the world flood; and the stormy voyage of Jonah, first swallowed by a whale and then delivered safely to shore.

But there also was time for lighter amusements. On clear days, after the sailors completed their work, the passengers were permitted to go above deck. There the children could run and stretch their legs. They especially delighted in watching playful porpoises circling the ship and huge whales spouting fountains of water into the air.

As the journey continued, the weather worsened. Violent west winds tossed the ship as if it were a cork

Mayflower II, *an exact replica of the original ship, in full sail*

bobbing on the sea. Riding the crest of giant waves, the ship would then plunge into the deep trough below. Waves crashed across the decks. During these storms, the passengers could only sit terrified in their quarters.

During one of the storms, curiosity took a young man, John Howland, out onto the main deck, something that was strictly forbidden in bad weather. A huge wave struck the ship and pitched the boy overboard. As he fell over, he grabbed the end of a rope hanging over the *Mayflower*'s side. When the ship rose on the next wave, he was slammed against the ship's side, but there a boat hook pierced his leather jacket and held him while he was hauled back aboard. The incident made the passengers

Mayflower *during a bad storm*

understand only too well why the shipmaster ordered them to stay below in stormy weather.

One day during another storm, a major disaster struck. One of the ship's main beams buckled. The force of the wind was so great and the thrashing of the sea so terrible that everyone feared the ship might break apart.

Some people advised turning back. Others urged going on. Even the crew was undecided. Then someone remembered a big iron jack that the Pilgrims had brought to use in building their new homes. The jack could brace the beam and support the upper decks. Hauling the jack out, the men found a firm footing under the cracked beam. Then they slowly turned the jack until it bit the oak beam and lifted it back into place. The ship was safe to journey on.

And once, in a break in a storm's howling wind, a small cry was heard: a baby boy had been born! His parents named him Oceanus, a name they thought fitting for a baby born at sea. But the birth of Oceanus did not add to the passenger count, for one person died during the voyage.

If the weather made life difficult, living conditions only added to the passengers' miseries. Below deck it was dark, damp, and smelly. With no place to bathe or do laundry, people wore the same clothes day and night for weeks on end. There were no fresh fruits or vegetables. Often the only food was dried meat, fish, or cheese and hardtack, small hard biscuits. Children could only sit quietly and play a few games while adults could only dream of the future. Time passed slowly as the weeks went by, and no one was sure how much longer the ship would be at sea. Nor did anyone know how long they would have to depend on the small supply of food after they reached land. To save food for the upcoming winter in the New World, everyone's rations were cut. Now hunger was added to the passengers' discomforts.

4
Arriving in America

The Pilgrims had discussed, planned, worked, and negotiated for three years to get to the New World. Now, nearly 3,000 miles and 67 days after they left England, the lookout in the crow's-nest called, "Land ho!" Everyone rushed on deck and stared into the horizon. Slowly a long dark line appeared between the sea and sky.

"Land! Land at last!" everyone cried. That day the Pilgrims thanked God with a special fervor. William Bradford wrote in his journal, "...they fell upon their knees and blessed the God of heaven who had brought them over the vast and furious sea."

But the *Mayflower* was not approaching Virginia, as had been the plan. The storm had blown the ship farther north. When Master Jones studied his maps, he discovered that the ship was nearing Cape Cod of New England. When English seafarers had explored the area some years earlier, they named it Cape Cod from the abundance of codfish in the water.

The ship's master called a meeting of the Pilgrim leaders, who were in the position of authority over the passengers. When told where they were, the Pilgrims insisted that the ship turn and head south. Their patent, or agreement, said Virginia, and they wished to abide by it. Master Jones agreed, but, unfortunately, he was not familiar with New England waters. The ship soon was caught between dangerous breakers and shoals where powerful currents threatened shipwreck on a sandbar. "Pray as you have never prayed before," the master urged the Pilgrims. Only a strong south wind could save the *Mayflower*.

A strong south wind did come up. The master steered into safer waters and suggested returning to Cape Cod. The Pilgrims agreed, but the decision created an urgent situation. New England was out of the jurisdiction of the Virginia Company. That meant the *Mayflower* passengers would not be governed by their patent from the Virginia Company. The Pilgrims would need some other plan of government. Such a governing pact was especially necessary because there were several different groups of people on the *Mayflower*, and they weren't always in agreement on their goals.

Before the *Mayflower* anchored, the Pilgrim leaders met and wrote an agreement declaring that all those signing it would work together for the common good, pass

Pilgrims signing the Mayflower Compact while still on the Mayflower

just laws, and elect and obey governing officials. All the men on the ship signed the document. Called the Mayflower Compact, it was one of the most important documents in American history. It was the first time that a group of colonists had ever made independent plans to govern themselves. And the document was based on the idea of the separation of church and state. A political office in the colony could not be filled by an officer of the church. John Carver was chosen the first governor of the group.

With the compact duly signed, the *Mayflower* was brought safely to anchor in Cape Cod Bay on the morning of November 11, 1620. Life in the New World was beginning for the *Mayflower* Pilgrims.

5

A Spot to Settle

Imagine arriving on a fictional other planet. It's cold and you have no place to go. You're faced by a wilderness that has neither people nor buildings. Or perhaps people do live there, but you've heard tales of their unfriendliness.

For the Pilgrims, they might just as well have arrived on another planet when they came to America. They were met by just such a cold, unpeopled wilderness, no more than a thick forest where icy winds swept through leafless trees.

But by noon of the *Mayflower*'s arrival, 16 men from the ship were headed toward the foreign shore. Because of the shallow water in the bay, the *Mayflower* had to anchor nearly a mile from shore. To get to land, the men used a longboat, a type of small boat carried by merchant ships to perform small operations. The men went to explore the land in hopes of finding a suitable site for settlement. Discovering fresh water springs, the men filled their kegs, and then cut a large load of juniper wood for the ship's cook. When they returned to the *Mayflower*, everyone crowded around them, wanting to know if the

The first wash day for the Pilgrims after they arrived in America

land was safe. The passengers were eager to go ashore and at last feel solid earth beneath them.

The Pilgrims spent the next day, the Sabbath, in prayer and rest, as was then their custom. But first thing Monday morning, the women loaded the boat with piles of dirty clothes and went ashore to do their long-overdue laundry. The women washed all morning and hung the clothes over bushes and low tree limbs to dry.

The children were also permitted to go ashore. They were only too happy to run and play after being cooped up for more than two months. When the clothes were dry, the Pilgrims loaded up the boat and headed back to the *Mayflower*. Until a settlement place was found and buildings built, the ship would serve as the Pilgrims' base.

For almost a month after, the men made exploratory trips on Cape Cod in search of a favorable site. On one of the trips, it was so cold and windy that a steady spray of water settled and froze on the men's clothes as they sailed along the shore. Their clothes became like stiff coats of glass. On another expedition, the men saw Native Americans but didn't get to meet them. The cautious natives ran away. The men also found other evidence of natives living in the area: mounds of dirt with baskets of corn hidden in them. The men struggled with their consciences about whether to take the corn, but the *Mayflower*'s food supply was getting dangerously low. The men decided to take the corn, certain that they would generously repay the natives at the earliest convenience. The corn later saved the Pilgrims from starvation. The Pilgrims later also amply repaid the natives.

The exploring teams learned a great deal about the land, the animals, and the resources of the area, but neither the first nor the second trips located a suitable place to settle. For one, the colonists needed a site near a harbor deep enough for the *Mayflower*—and, later, trading ships—to be anchored. And the site would have to be suitable for agriculture and be high enough to hold a good lookout point against possible enemies.

The third expedition produced a frightening encounter with some natives, and it ran into violent winter weather, but it also located the Pilgrims' new home. The men found Plymouth, a place that Master John Smith had called by that name on his earlier expedition along the coast. It had a harbor fit for shipping and fields cleared of trees. Someone had evidently lived there at one time, but now the land appeared abandoned. The men fished in the streams and hunted game, pleased to find a place so abundant in wildlife.

When the men got back to the *Mayflower*, they announced that the colonists' search was over. The news was met with happiness and relief, but the people on the ship had a tragic report to make in return. William Bradford's wife, Dorothy, had fallen overboard and drowned. Some thought that she had perhaps taken her own life, seeing the hardships that lay ahead in the New World, or from grief over the small son left behind in Leyden. She and her husband had left the child for good keeping with friends until such a time as he could safely join his parents in America.

But there was also better news aboard the *Mayflower*: another baby boy had been born. His parents called him Peregrine, which means "wanderer or pilgrim." Everyone thought it a good name for the first Pilgrim child born in New England.

6

A Tragic First Winter

On December 16, 1620, a group of Pilgrims left the *Mayflower*, sailed toward land in their boat, and stepped ashore on the spot that the exploratory group had chosen to be their home. The exact place was what we now call Plymouth Rock.

The men immediately began making plans. For protection, they would build a gun platform overlooking the bay. They had already chosen Miles Standish as their military commander. The men would also build a Common House that would be used to store things and to house some of the people until other homes could be built. The Common House would later become the meeting house. Individual homes would follow for the 19 family groups into which the passengers had been divided. Single men were assigned to the family groups. A small contingent of workers stayed ashore in a little camp to start the building project and to guard it. The other workers returned to the *Mayflower* at the end of each day of work.

The Common House had barely been completed when tragedy struck. Some people started getting sick with

Plymouth Rock

Pilgrims building their homes in America

scurvy, a disease caused by a lack of the vitamins in fruits and vegetables. There were no native berries, fruits, or greens at that time of year, and by then the people hadn't had fresh food for about four months.

The Pilgrims called scurvy and other diseases the Great Sickness. Sometimes they caused death in a day's time. People of all ages died. During the worst time, two or three people died each day. Entire families were wiped out, and few families survived intact. The Billington and Hopkins families were two of them. When children became orphans, they were accepted into other households.

Many of those who survived were weakened. Unaccustomed to the harsh climate, hard labor, and miserable living conditions, they then fell ill with pneumonia. There was little medicine. Except for the six or seven people who were well enough to care for the others, not much could be done for the ill. Only about half of the colonists survived that first winter in their new home.

The settlers buried their dead at night on a hill in unmarked graves. They were afraid that the natives in the area, seeing so many graves, would realize that the number of colonists was greatly reduced.

The weather remained a wintry cold through January and February. The few men who were not sick continued to cut down trees and build houses. Food was running out, but the colonists found some hope by observing from the fallen leaves that an abundance of fruit and nut trees grew in the area. They also were grateful that the forest was filled with game, and the waters were rich in fish. Unfortunately, the Pilgrims had not brought the right kind of hooks from England to be able to catch all of the available fish.

March arrived. It appeared that the Sickness was about over. Fewer people were becoming ill. As the air started to get warm, the doors of the Common House were thrown open, and the sick began to gain strength. It was spring. The remaining Pilgrims thanked God for bringing them through the winter and asked for blessing during the planting season ahead.

7

A Hopeful Spring

Luckily, spring came early in 1621. Although about half of the colonists had died during the winter, the warm spring days brought renewed hope and courage to those who survived. The colonists could now turn to spring planting. Each family would have a small kitchen garden for its own use, raising peas, beans, and other crops from seeds brought from England. Outside the village, there would be a large, 20-acre community cornfield. Everyone would share the work of cultivating and tending crops.

Spring was also the time of house building. The men cut trees and made boards and worked earnestly in building homes for the individual families. Each home had a fireplace for cooking and for winter heating. Roofs were made of thatch, a reedlike grass that grew nearby. While thatch made thick roofs that provided warmth, rain came through them sometimes. Fire was another danger to thatch roofs. After the roofs dried, sparks from the chimney could set them afire.

Home furnishings were simple. There had been little space on the *Mayflower* for bringing chairs, tables, or beds, so the settlers had to make their own furniture.

Pilgrims using thatch to make a roof for their home

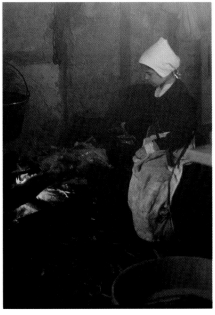

Pilgrim woman preparing a meal for her family

They nailed together boards to make stools and benches. Beds were crude, with ropes crisscrossing the frame to support a mattress, a big bag stuffed with feathers, rags, or even cattails. The older children usually slept on the floor or in the house's loft. The small children slept in trundle beds that were pushed under the parents' bed in the daytime to save space. The rooms were too small for tables. At meals, people sat on benches.

Many utensils were made of wood because very little iron or metal was available. Meals were served on wooden plates with wooden spoons. People ate with their fingers and drank from wooden mugs or from tankards made of leather. Even bottles were made of leather. Only the utensils used directly over the fire were made of iron.

Each family had a large kettle that was used for cooking and for other household chores. Soapmaking was an unpleasant task because the soap mixture smelled bad. Soap was made from household fats and grease and from lye, a substance made from wood ashes.

Candlemaking was not quite as unwelcome a task. A rod with strings attached to it was dipped into a kettle of grease called tallow, a kind of animal fat. After several dippings, the strings were covered with layers of tallow and were hung on a rack to dry. The colonists added bayberries to make the candles smell better and burn longer.

Life in the Plymouth colony was not easy. What items had not been brought from England had to be made in the village. If they couldn't be made with the few materials available, people did without.

8

Helpful Visitors

One morning in March, a Native American walked into the Plymouth village. His presence caused great alarm, for the colonists had never seen a native face to face. In spite of the cool weather, he wore only a small piece of leather from his waist, which greatly embarrassed the modest Pilgrims. The visitor greeted the settlers in English. He said his name was Samoset and that he had learned English from some Englishmen who fished along the coast.

When the Pilgrims realized that Samoset came in peace, they asked him many questions. He told the Pilgrims all about the native tribes in the area, and which were friendly and which were not. He himself had lived in the area for about eight months, but now his home was a day's sail away. He was visiting the Wampanoag tribe, some 40 miles away. He told the Pilgrims why few natives were in their neighborhood. Several years before, the Patuxet tribe, which had lived there, had all died from an epidemic. That explained why the colonists had found meadows and fields cleared but unplanted.

The Pilgrims were pleased to spend the afternoon talking to Samoset. They were learning much about their new home. In appreciation and hospitality, the settlers offered him a variety of foods to eat, but they intended their welcome to end there. They wished him to leave before the day was over, feeling unsure about having an unknown native spend the night with them. But the talkative Samoset was not willing to go. At last he was lodged for the night in one of the houses, but a night guard was posted to keep watch for any trouble. As it turned out, the night was quite peaceful. By early morning, Samoset was ready to go. Before he left, the colonists gave him a knife, a bracelet, and a ring. He promised to come again in a day or two with some neighboring natives, as well as some beaver skins to trade. The colonists were eager to set up trade with the natives.

A few days later he did return with a friend, Tisquantum, or Squanto, as he came to be known. Squanto, a Patuxet, had lived on the site of the village until 15 years ago. Then he was taken captive by an English exploring team and sold into slavery in Spain. Later he lived in England for several years, where he learned English.

Massasoit

When Squanto returned to America, he discovered that his entire tribe had been wiped out by the epidemic. He was the last Patuxet. He, too, would have died if he hadn't have been taken to England.

Because of his excellent English, Squanto acted as interpreter between the colonists and the Native Americans. He introduced the Pilgrims to Massasoit, Chief of the Wampanoags. The chief and the Pilgrims exchanged gifts amidst great ceremony and then made an important peace treaty. By its terms, Massasoit's people would not hurt or steal from the colonists. Offenders would be punished and stolen goods returned. Furthermore, the natives and the colonists would come to each other's aid if anyone unjustly warred against them. Massasoit was to send word of the treaty to his neighbors and allies, so that they would not hurt the people of the new settlement.

The treaty was kept for 55 years.

9

A Bountiful Time

In April, the *Mayflower* at last sailed back to England. The master had delayed leaving because some of his crew had fallen ill, and a number of them died. But the kindly master had also stayed to help the colonists. His ship had served as the people's base until they were able to construct some buildings, and it also served as a hospital during the Great Sickness. Seeing the enormous hardships that the Pilgrims faced, he offered to take any of them back to England without charge, but all the settlers chose to remain in their new home.

In the spring, Squanto came to live with the Pilgrims. He said he was comfortable with English-speaking people and wanted to help them. The Pilgrims believed that he was "a special instrument of God for [our] good." And indeed, Squanto was the best of friends and an excellent teacher to the settlers. Many of them were inexperienced with country living and even with agriculture. Many had had indoor jobs in Leyden.

Squanto knew how to fish by native methods. He knew which wild herbs and greens were good to eat and which made useful medicines. He also knew how to grow

Squanto taught the Pilgrims how to plant corn.

corn, which was a valuable item because it was the chief food in the area and also was used as money in trading.

Squanto taught the colonists that corn should not be planted in rows, but in little hills a few feet apart. Three little fish should be buried in each hill to serve as fertilizer. He told the Pilgrims what was the best time for planting: when the oak leaves were the same size as a mouse's ear. He taught them to plant pumpkins between the corn hills. The big pumpkin leaves would shade the ground, keeping it moist and free of weeds. And if beans were planted in the corn hills, the cornstalks would serve as bean poles. The colonists followed Squanto's instructions and had an excellent crop.

Squanto also taught the men how to make traps and snares and how to skin and dress the game they caught.

The children liked Squanto and followed him around. He told them stories of his childhood and taught them secrets of the forest, streams, and wild animals.

By the end of the summer, the Pilgrims were enjoying robust health, and their gardens had produced all the food they'd need for the coming winter. They also had caught many fish and waterfowl, dried them for later use, and had stored venison, wild turkeys, and other game. Berries and fruits were dried and packed away, too, insuring against a return of scurvy.

One of the few sad notes of the summer was the death of Governor Carver. While working in the field one day, he fell ill and died a few days later. William Bradford was then elected governor, an office he held for 36 years. A wise and just leader, Governor Bradford's service to his fellow colonists ended only with his death in 1657. It was he who helped them organize the first Harvest Feast. The Pilgrims wanted to give special thanks to God for the blessings they had received during their first year in

The First Thanksgiving

Plymouth. They decided to hold a harvest festival that fall, when Massasoit and 90 of his tribe were to pay a visit.

Massasoit's men brought a gift of five deer and some wild turkeys to the feast. The meat was roasted on great fires built in the open. The few Pilgrim wives who had survived the previous winter made cornbread and huge kettles of stew. When the time came to partake of the rich feast, Elder Brewster said a heartfelt prayer of thanksgiving. For though the Pilgrims had endured untold hardships, they had also found helpful friends in the Native Americans, built 11 buildings, started in the fur trade, and stored up a bountiful harvest for the second winter.

The Pilgrims and their guests ate abundantly at the feast. In fact, it lasted three days. Between meals, the native and Pilgrim women exchanged information about babies and food; the children ran races and played games; and the men held shooting contests, pitting Pilgrim muskets against native bows and arrows. And there was much singing and dancing though only the natives danced. The Pilgrims looked upon dancing as ungodly, but they tolerated it in their New World neighbors. They were grateful that these natives, once feared as savages, had turned out to be generous and willing friends who literally had helped the inexperienced newcomers survive. They believed it fitting that these new friends should share what would later be called the nation's first Thanksgiving.

10

A Visit to Plymouth

Plymouth has been called "America's Hometown." Much of American history and tradition are rooted in the little New England village. It was in the Plymouth colony that religious freedom and self-government were born. And although it was not the first colony in America—Jamestown, Virginia came earlier—Plymouth serves as the symbolic birthplace of our nation.

Each year about one million people visit Plymouth, where numerous sites and museums preserve treasured pieces of our American heritage.

Plymouth Rock, recalling the Pilgrims' landing, is displayed in a large portico in Plymouth Harbor. It's the spot where the Pilgrims are supposed to have first stepped. Looking at the legendary stone brings back the emotional moment when our nation's courageous founders first greeted land after their long and harrowing pilgrimage.

Above the rock is Cole's Hill, which gives a panoramic view of Plymouth Harbor. The site also is where the colonists buried many of their members during their first tragic winter in America.

Portico over Plymouth Rock

A popular and thrilling stop is Plimoth Plantation, three miles from the center of town. It's a full-scale reconstruction of the original Pilgrim colony as it looked in 1627. No effort has been spared to present an exact picture of life at that time. Through dress, speech, manner, and attitude, the villagers—the guides and hostesses in the Plimoth village—portray the residents of the colony. The exhibits and activities follow the seasons in the farming community as it carries out all the tasks necessary for living—planting and harvesting crops, tending to animals, sawing lumber, preparing meals, weaving, making candles, and preserving food, to name a few. What you see will depend on the time you visit. But busy as they are all year long, the villagers are always eager for

Plimoth Plantation street scene

questions and conversation. What an exciting way to learn the story of the Pilgrims!

Nearby is the Wampanoag Indian Settlement, offering a sampling of the rich culture of the region's first inhabitants. Native people recreate the daily activities of their ancestors as well as the special events in their history, such as intertribal trading and Chief Massasoit's annual visit. You'll see the inside of a native dwelling and watch a tree carved out and made into a canoe.

Back in the town center, don't miss the Pilgrim Hall Museum, the country's oldest museum. It contains a collection of Pilgrim possessions—muskets, pots and other household utensils, and furniture.

Be sure to climb aboard the *Mayflower II*, the full-scale reproduction of the type of vessel that brought the

Plymouth National Wax Museum

Pilgrims to the New World. You'll see men and women, dressed in costume and using the dialect of the period, portray the passengers and crew. You can go below deck to see where the Pilgrims lived during their long voyage. Don't expect any of the modern conveniences that we take for granted!

None of the houses from the original settlement still exist, but several later ones do. The Richard Sparrow House, built in 1640, is the oldest house in Plymouth. The first floor is unchanged from its earliest days. Another popular early house is the Harlow Old Fort House. It's now a museum that features demonstrations of 17th-century Pilgrim activities, such as weaving, candlemaking, and spinning.

For another lifelike representation of the Pilgrim story, try the Plymouth National Wax Museum. In more than 20 detailed scenes—accompanied by light, sound, and animation—you'll learn how the Pilgrims were mistreated in England, then moved to Holland, and finally came to America. You'll also see Massasoit's men bringing deer to the "Harvest Feast."

With so many places to go, your feet may welcome a rest. The Plymouth Rock Trolley is a good way to do that—and to see some other unique sights in town. The driver explains the different monuments and buildings. Among the many special treats are the National Monument to the Forefathers, the largest granite monument in the country. There's also a statue of Massasoit overlooking Plymouth Harbor and a statue of the Pilgrim Mother, including a fountain. It's a memorial to the women of the *Mayflower;* their names are inscribed on the fountain.

The Plymouth area offers a variety of other interesting stops. At Cranberry World you can see how cranberries, abundant and native to the area, are grown and harvested. The Pilgrims didn't have cranberries at their first "Harvest Feast," but not long after, the natives introduced the colonists to the tart red berry that has come to be associated with Thanksgiving. The Edaville Railroad, a real steam train, is another way to ride through thousands of acres of cranberry country.

Back in Plymouth, a popular spot with many visitors is the town wharf. Fishing boats arrive daily with their catches of fish and lobsters. It's fun to watch as the fish are sorted according to size and shipped out. An abundance of fish for food made Plymouth a good place for the Pilgrims, too. Being right on the bay, Plymouth offers a variety of other water activities. Seagoing captains offer whale watch cruises and trips to Provincetown, near the *Mayflower*'s first anchoring. Deep-sea fishing excursions are fun, too. If you're in town in the summer, Plymouth's beautiful beach is great for swimming.

Plymouth is a town that may not be large, but it's huge for places to see and things to do. It'll give you a real sense of appreciation for our nation's Pilgrim settlers. The harbor where the courageous travelers first stepped and where another *Mayflower* now stands...the beautiful village and simple way of life that's perfectly recreated in Plimoth Plantation...the hill that provides a good lookout against possible enemies in the new land...these and so many of Plymouth's other offerings will help you recreate the home and lives of the determined people who valued freedom above all. They were the people who planted the seeds of freedom for us, too.

Index